MW00574775

THE WAY of LIFE

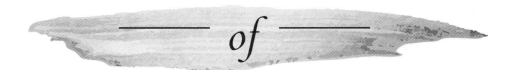

BILL JOHNSON

THE WAY *of* LIFE

EXPERIENCING
THE CULTURE OF
HEAVEN ON EARTH

© Copyright 2019–Bill Johnson

All rights reserved. This book is protected by the copyright laws of the United States of America. This book may not be copied or reprinted for commercial gain or profit. The use of short quotations or occasional page copying for personal or group study is permitted and encouraged. Permission will be granted upon request. Unless otherwise identified, Scripture quotations are taken from the New King James Version. Copyright © 1982 by Thomas Nelson, Inc. Used by permission. All rights reserved. Please note that Destiny Image's publishing style capitalizes certain pronouns in Scripture that refer to the Father, Son, and Holy Spirit, and may differ from some publishers' styles.

DESTINY IMAGE® PUBLISHERS, INC.

P.O. Box 310, Shippensburg, PA 17257-0310

"Promoting Inspired Lives."

This book and all other Destiny Image and Destiny Image Fiction books are available at Christian bookstores and distributors worldwide.

Cover design by Christian Rafetto

Interior design by Terry Clifton

For more information on foreign distributors, call 717-532-3040.

Reach us on the Internet: www.destinyimage.com.

ISBN 13 TP: 978-0-7684-4858-0

ebook ISBN: 978-0-7684-4859-7

For Worldwide Distribution, Printed in the U.S.A.

1 2 3 4 5 6 7 8 / 22 21 20 19

Hello!

I want to thank you for joining me in my course, *The Way of Life*. I've been changed by that simple phrase from Matthew 6, "on earth as it is in heaven." The kingdom of this world was made to be like the Kingdom of Heaven. Heaven on earth is God's dream! Our prayers are powerful and give occasion for God's heart to become the overwhelming influence over this world! That's why I created this course: to help you encounter and steward His Presence in new ways.

We need to create a culture where the things of God can thrive. Over the course of the next eight weeks, you will discover what it means to partner with His Presence and see the things not of God bow their knee to the name of Jesus.

Thank you again for taking the time to be with me. I pray that each lesson would give you the courage to run toward impossible situations in your life and release the supernatural solutions of Jesus!

Blessings,
Bill Johnson

CONTENTS

USING THE STUDY GUIDE

**This** study guide provides you with eight interactive sessions that you will go through together as a group or class. You may also engage the sessions individually, but you will get the most out of the curriculum content by engaging the sessions in a small group or class experience.

In order to prepare yourself to foster revival in your community, you need reinforcement. The keys that Bill provides in both the book and curriculum materials are designed for practical application in your daily life.

In the exercises you will have journaling space follow each of the questions. As you engage each of the exercises, we pray that you will encounter the supernatural power of God and that you will continue to be transformed by the Holy Spirit as a growing disciple who learns how to sustain the power and purity of God in your everyday life.

Session One

THE GREAT COMMISSION

Jesus commissioned us to pray that it would be on Earth as it is in Heaven, which means it must be possible. We pray "Our Father" because the Great Commission is part of our collective, cultural identity as a church family. God's Kingdom comes when we have been deeply moved by His heart. Our prayers are powerful and give occasion for God's heart and world to become the overwhelming influence over this world!

JOURNAL

Week 1

VIDEO LISTENING GUIDE

1. In the Lord's Prayer, perhaps more aptly described as the _____'s prayer, Jesus commissions us to pray "On _____ as it is in _____."

2. We call God "_____ Father," which speaks to our _____ identity.

3. Our breakthrough is initiated by our _____.

4. You _____ not because you _____ not. It's possible to be in lack because of _____.

5. To know God's dreams, you have to know His _____.

Summary

Heaven on Earth is God's dream! This week's lesson focuses on Jesus' commission to us, His disciples, to pray for Heaven to fill the world around us. When we understand that Jesus' prayers are God's dreams for the world, we can more effectively partner with Him to create a Kingdom reality on Earth as it is in Heaven.

The Disciple's Prayer

Though frequently called The Lord's Prayer, the prayer Jesus encourages us to pray in Matthew 6 may more accurately called "The Disciple's Prayer." As followers of Jesus, we have the opportunity to lean in to God's destiny for Earth, seeing measurable answers to this prayer in our lives and in our world as we establish His dominion alongside Him!

Discussion Questions

1. As a follower of Jesus, what do you think is your role in creating a culture of Heaven in the world around you?

_____

_____

_____

_____

_____

_____

---

2. What does God's desire for the Earth to become like Heaven reveal to you about His heart and character?

---

3. What are some practical ways you can tap into God's dreams for humanity and the Earth?

_____

_____

_____

_____

4. Knowing that God wants to involve you in His destiny for mankind, how does your sense of personal calling or purpose change?

_____

_____

_____

_____

_____

_____

_____

_____

_____

_____

_____

_____

The Semantics

Every aspect of Jesus' prayer in Matthew 6 reveals a unique and powerful aspect of God's heart and our identity in Him. When we reflect on and study the specific language Jesus chose for this prayer, we can gain a deeper understanding of who He is and the destiny He has called us to, both as a church and individually.

5. Why is it so significant that Jesus instructs us to pray "Our Father" versus simply "Father"?

_____

_____

_____

_____

_____

_____

_____

_____

_____

_____

6. What role does worship play in our ability to see Heaven flood the Earth?

_____

_____

_____

_____

_____

_____

_____

_____

_____

7. How is God's role as King influential in the prayer for Heaven to come on Earth? What would it look like if His Kingship was fully established here?

_____

_____

_____

_____

_____

_____

_____

_____

_____

Activation: Celebrating Your Role as Disciple

Spend time in groups of two to three, and pray the "Disciple's Prayer" out loud together.

How did God shift or awaken your heart to the true meaning of this prayer?

Does anything stand out or specifically resonate with you?

Share with one another any revelations you experienced or insights you gleaned.

Video Listening Guide Answer Key:

1. Disciple, Earth, Heaven

2. Our, cultural

3. Faith

4. Have, ask, prayerlessness

5. Prayers

Great work! You've completed week one. Let's move on to our next week, where we will explore answers to prayers!

Session Two

ANSWERS TO PRAYER

Freedom doesn't mean I do what I want; it means I have the ability to do what is right. Purity is less about doing things for God and more about how we represent Him. The power of Christ enables us to move past our personal weakness.

JOURNAL

Week 2

VIDEO LISTENING GUIDE

1. _____ and _____ are the two most important ways we demonstrate the Kingdom.

2. Purity is the _____ and _____ of Christ formed in _____.

3. Our _____ doesn't come by self-_____ but by being immersed in God's _____.

4. _____ is necessary to demonstrate the miracle _____ of Jesus.

5. The power of God helps us overcome personal _____.

Summary

If we are called to bring Heaven to life all around us, then we need to create a culture where the things of God can thrive. By pursuing the two core values of power and purity, we can cultivate rich soil for the Kingdom, seeing the will of God unfold both corporately and in our individual lives.

Walking in Purity

When we walk in purity, we demonstrate the beauty of Jesus. Living purely isn't about following rules or measuring up, but beholding who God is and being transformed by His Presence. By deeply seeking and understanding the heart of God, we can become accurate portrayals of His character and nature to everyone we come in contact with!

Discussion Questions

1. Though we are called to purity, God also desires that we live in freedom. How do purity and freedom go hand in hand?

----

2. Pastor Bill shares that "when we see Him, we become like Him." Why is beholding Jesus so important to our spiritual development?

3. Why do you think holiness has gotten a "bad rap" in the church? How is God changing that in our day?

---

4. What does it mean for you to pursue purity in your everyday life? What might God be speaking to you about cultivating His character?

Walking in Power

Just like purity, power is a necessary ingredient to demonstrating the values of the Lord's Kingdom. Jesus demonstrated a life of power perfectly, and He tells us we will accomplish even greater things than He did! When we tune into all He has done and all He wants to do in our lives and the lives of those we encounter, we can create an empowered culture where the supernatural becomes natural.

1. Jesus was motivated by compassion when He healed, but His miracles and ministry have another layer. Why is it so important that power doesn't end with compassion?

_____

_____

_____

_____

_____

_____

_____

_____

_____

_____

2. How does God's power help us overcome personal weakness, and how is weakness distinct from "sin nature"?

_____

_____

_____

_____

_____

_____

_____

_____

3. What does it mean to "quench the Spirit"? What role does pursuing God's Presence play in this?

_____

_____

_____

_____

_____

Activation: Identifying Our Blind Spots

If possible, have praise and worship music ready to go—either live, or on some kind of audio system.

Spend time individually journaling about the concept of overcoming personal weakness through God's power.

While our sin nature has been overcome by the blood of Jesus, there may be areas He wants to give us a greater measure of freedom.

Ask Him where He wants to apply His power so you can reflect His beauty to the world. What are one or two practical ways you can pursue this in your everyday life?

Video Listening Guide Answer Key:

1. Power, purity

2. Nature, character, me

3. Transformation, determination, presence

4. Power, love

5. Weakness

Congratulations! You made it through week two. Are you ready to move forward and learn more about the culture of Heaven?

Session Three

CORNERSTONES OF THOUGHT

Creating a culture where the Kingdom can thrive is the first step of Kingdom living. If we really believe God is good, His goodness will manifest in every area of our lives. We are called to trust God in both times of abundance and struggle and our behaviors give evidence to what we truly believe.

JOURNAL

Week 3

VIDEO LISTENING GUIDE

1. The revelation of God's _____ is the invitation to _____.

2. _____ explores what the revelation of God's goodness provides.

3. What we _____ has to affect our behavior.

4. Jesus trusted and believed that everything was His and His _____ was locked.

5. When we have discovered our call, no _____ is too _____.

Summary

How can we see the things Jesus saw? What does it take to implement Heaven's values on Earth? There are four cornerstone beliefs that facilitate the mind of Christ, which will overflow into our actions: God is good, nothing is impossible, Jesus' blood paid for everything, and everyone is significant. If we truly believe these things, Kingdom living will be our default, and we will have all the tools we need to see Heaven manifest around us!

Culture Shift

Every great company has an on-boarding process for employees to learn about company culture. To be successful and unified in our pursuits, we have to be on the same page about core values. We have to be of a similar mind if we want to move forward together! The same principle holds true in our pursuit of the Kingdom in measurable ways.

Discussion Questions

1. Why is it so crucial for the culture of Heaven to begin inside of us before we fulfill the Great Commission in broader ways?

_____

_____

_____

_____

2. How does the Lord train us in the ways of the Kingdom?

_____

_____

_____

_____

_____

_____

_____

_____

3. What is our role in adopting a heavenly mindset?

_____

_____

_____

Heaven's Core Values

All organizations have a mission and vision statement guiding their endeavors. By understanding what motivates a brand, employees can do their jobs effectively and in unity. Following Jesus is no exception! The four values discussed in this lesson are principles that should guide the thought processes and actions of all believers, resulting in real Kingdom advancement in all we do.

1. How is God's goodness related to our ability to dream big?

------

2. What would our lives (and our world!) look like if we truly believed nothing is impossible?

------

3. How is it possible that we can hold on to hope even when our life circumstances don't seem favorable?

------

4. Even in the midst of pain, how was Jesus able to serve humanity by dying on the cross?

Activation: Thankfulness for the Glory

Spend time in small groups of two to three and discuss what it means to dream with the Lord.

How is dreaming with God a part of seeing His Kingdom manifest on this side of Heaven?

Share specific dreams you have with one another, and how God might use them to advance the Kingdom.

To finish, pray over one another, that you would believe nothing is impossible as you place your faith in Jesus!

Video Listening Guide Answer Key:

1. Goodness, dream

2. Faith

3. Believe

4. Destiny

5. Position, low

God is doing amazing things! We can't wait to jump into next week's lesson with you.

Session Four

THE ADVANCING KINGDOM

Worship is the offering of ourselves; when we give ourselves to God, He always comes with fire. Stirring revival isn't the responsibility of church leaders; it's up to each one of us to sustain the fire God starts. Until everyone's shadow heals the sick, we aren't fully where God wants us to be, but He will renew our faith so we can turn from dead works and walk in power.

NOTES

Week 4

VIDEO LISTENING GUIDE

1. No revival ended because of _____, but because of _____.

2. God lights the _____, but the priests keep it _____.

3. In worship, the gift we offer is _____.

4. Never do superior _____ come from an inferior _____.

5. We owe the world a _____ that is influenced by God's _____.

Summary

The nature of God is that He always moves from glory to glory. We have the privilege of joining Him in His mission, stirring revival culture with our worship. When we offer ourselves to Him, He pours out His glory and radiance, and we are empowered to embody these things in our daily lives. This is the heart of Kingdom advancement and revival: A rich, worshipful relationship with God!

What Is Revival?

Like any fire does, all corporate revival starts with an individual spark. Our transforming encounters with God pave the way for us to carry His heart into the world, igniting a culture of revival that magnifies His Presence. When we make it our mission to know God and make Him known, He can do powerful things with our lives!

Discussion Questions

1. How do we know that God doesn't intend for revival to end?

_____

_____

_____

_____

_____

_____

_____

_____

_____

_____

2. Why is worship such a powerful tool in igniting and sustaining revival?

_____

_____

_____

_____

_____

_____

_____

_____

_____

3. What is the difference between praise, thanksgiving, and worship?

_____

_____

_____

_____

_____

_____

_____

_____

_____

_____

Beholding God

Like revival, seeing the Kingdom manifest in our lives and in the world begins with knowing God. Think of it this way: In order to effectively minister God's heart, it's crucial that we know Him. When we behold who He is, we can become like Him and put His power and love on display for all to see and experience!

1. How does seeing God for who He is transform us and empower us to act like Him?

_____

_____

_____

_____

_____

_____

_____

2. What does God tell us about our ability to do works like Jesus?

3. What is the true meaning of "repent"?

_____

_____

_____

_____

_____

_____

4. How does faith affect our ability and capacity to "see" with God's perspective?

_____

_____

_____

_____

_____

_____

_____

_____

_____

_____

_____

Activation: A Countenance like His

If possible, have praise and worship music ready to go—either live, or on some kind of audio system.

Spend time individually, reflecting on one of the four cornerstones of thought and ask the Lord which one He wants you to focus on in your life.

1. God is good.

2. Nothing is impossible.

3. The blood of Jesus paid for everything.

4. Everyone is significant.

How could this revelation and heart transformation bring a bit of Heaven into the world?

Ask God what beliefs you've had that have made this cornerstone not feel true for you. Ask God to help you walk out in this belief and to see measurable impact on your life as you become more like Him.

Share with the group what the Lord showed you.

Video Listening Guide Answer Key:

1. Excess, lack

2. Fire, burning

3. Ourselves

4. Blessings, covenant

5. Countenance, countenance

Are you ready for more? We're so expectant that God will meet us in next week's lesson!

Session Five

ERASING THE LINES

Truths imparted deeply in us change everything about us. When we learn what the Kingdom looks like, God empowers us to influence the world. Every believer is a priest unto the Lord, so there is no vocation or calling that's more valuable or important. Everything we do can be a sacred assignment from God. We contribute in the most significant and powerful ways when we are free to follow the dreams of our hearts.

JOURNAL

_____

_____

_____

_____

_____

_____

_____

_____

_____

_____

_____

_____

_____

_____

_____

_____

_____

_____

_____

Week 5

VIDEO LISTENING GUIDE

1. The principles of the Kingdom are _____ to any sphere of life.

2. There is no divide between _____ and _____.

3. Our strength is in the _____ who called us, not in our titles.

4. God adds blessing and prosperity without _____.

5. The _____ of God always rests upon our _____.

Summary

While the world may draw a line between the sacred and secular, God doesn't categorize our lives that way. Because all believers are priests unto the Lord, anything we do in faith can be consecrated unto Him. Whether we are working at our jobs or serving overseas, we can be ambassadors of the Kingdom in every sphere of our lives.

Kingdom Without Boundaries

God's values aren't meant to stay in the church. He invites us and empowers us to bring His value system into everything we do. As Pastor Bill teaches, the patterns and mindsets we learn from the Lord are transferable everywhere. With this mindset, we can appreciate vocations and callings outside the traditional "ministry" approach.

Discussion Questions

1. Why is it limiting for us to create lines between the sacred and secular?

_____

_____

_____

_____

_____

_____

_____

_____

---

2. How can we effectively bring the Kingdom into our spheres of influence?

---

3. How does God consecrate our assignments as "ministry" even if we don't work in church or serve overseas as a missionary?

---

4. What does Pastor Bill mean when He says we can look for the uniqueness of God in our roles and callings?

Blessings as Resources

While material wealth isn't the goal of the believer, God desires to equip us with abundance so we have the resources we need to bless others and live generously. Along the same lines, God can use our success and abundance to inspire and empower others.

1. How does our success and anointing in a specific area bring the Kingdom in our sphere of influence?

   _____

   _____

   _____

   _____

   _____

   _____

   _____

   _____

2. Why is it so important that believers are equipped materially, and what is the Kingdom balance between materialism and God-given abundance?

   _____

   _____

_____

_____

_____

_____

_____

_____

_____

_____

3. What is the significance of the Promised Land in terms of trusting God to supply for our needs?

_____

_____

_____

_____

_____

_____

_____

_____

_____

_____

Activation: Resources for Success

Spend time in small groups of two to three and discuss the relationship between Heavenly wealth and our role as Kingdom stewards.

Share specific areas where God has challenged you to trust Him more deeply to bring resource and blessings.

Then, pray over one other in faith that the Lord will supply every need, declaring His desire for abundant life for each one of us!

Video Listening Guide Answer Key:

1. Transferable

2. Sacred, secular

3. Person

4. Sorrow

5. Fire, sacrifice

Can you believe we're already five weeks in? We are continually praying that the Lord would reveal powerful truths about His Kingdom to you.

Session Six

JESUS: UNAFRAID OF THE SECULAR

We are called as apostles to shape and transform culture as we partner with the Spirit, like Paul. The Lord's ideas and the principles of the Kingdom are transferable to every aspect of culture. Jesus calls us the salt of the Earth, which means He wants to evenly distribute us to add flavor to the world and bring Heaven to Earth.

JOURNAL

VIDEO LISTENING GUIDE

Week 6

1. The word "apostle" means "_____ _____."

2. The Lord's ideas are _____ to secular _____.

3. Jesus tells us that wherever _____ or _____ are gathered in His _____, He is there!

4. In the New Covenant, the _____ influences the ungodly, not the other way around.

5. God changed Saul's name to _____ to equate His _____ with His _____.

Summary

In many areas, Jesus built His church upon secular principles. While this may be surprising, it's important to remember that in the New Covenant, the godly influences the ungodly, not the other way around. This means we can be salt and light, adding Kingdom flavor to the culture around us! Because Jesus isn't afraid of "secular" culture, He can equip us to be powerful examples and servants like Paul and Barnabas.

Living as "Sent Ones"

The word "apostle" means "sent one," which speaks volumes of our identity as disciples. God sends each one of us into culture with powerful influence and gives us the tools we need to function as salt in our own areas of influence. Whether you are a stay-at-home parent, a business person, a creative, or an evangelist, you have profound anointing wherever you are because the Spirit lives in you.

Discussion Questions

1. Why is it so significant that Jesus used a secular concept to define apostleship and church?

_____

_____

_____

_____

_____

_____

---

2. When you think about the term "sent one," what functions or traits come to mind? What does this say about your calling and identity as an apostle?

---

3. What does the analogy of salt illustrate about our calling as disciples?

The Example of Paul

When we look at scripture, God gave each one of His disciples a unique anointing to carry His message into the world. The apostle Paul is a perfect example of how a believer can effectively minister in secular culture.

1. What was the symbolism behind Saul's name change to "Paul"?

_____

_____

_____

_____

_____

_____

2. Why did Paul have such a powerful impact on the Romans to whom he
   was bringing the gospel?

_____

_____

_____

_____

_____

_____

_____

_____

_____

_____

3. Why do you think so many of us are hesitant to be engaged with culture? And why isn't Jesus afraid of it?

_____

_____

_____

_____

_____

_____

_____

_____

_____

_____

Activation: Your Apostolic Calling

Take time individually to reflect upon your unique calling to be apostolic, asking God where He might be sending you. Are you, like Paul, called to reveal God in secular culture? In what capacity?

Then get into groups of two and spend time praying for your unique roles in ushering in God's Kingdom on Earth. Ask the Holy Spirit for practical action steps for walking in your calling powerfully as Paul did, as well as vision for what your next steps are in your calling.

Video Listening Guide Answer Key:

1. Sent one

2. Relevant, culture

3. Two, three, name

4. Godly

5. Paul, role, calling

You're doing so well! Next week, we will cover how everything we do can be done unto the Lord.

Session Seven

Unto the Lord

When we follow Jesus, every part of our day can be a profound chance to see and worship the Lord. We are called to do all things, no matter how mundane, with all our might as unto the Lord. All things have spiritual ramifications! No matter what our vocation, we are all walking in God's divine design for our lives.

JOURNAL

Week 7

VIDEO LISTENING GUIDE

1. When God is _____ _____, there is no _____ _____.

2. Everything in our lives can be an expression of _____.

3. We are called to deposit the _____ of Jesus into everyone around us!

4. When Queen Sheba saw Solomon's stairs, she said "There is a _____ in Israel!"

5. Because we are walking with God in His design, there is no _____ part of life!

Summary

What if every area of your life could be infused with purpose? When we partner with the Lord in believing there is no "ordinary" aspect of life, we can experience fresh joy and meaning. As a "sent one," you have powerful, eternal impact in everything you do, wherever you do it!

No Number Two

The principles of God's Kingdom defy our understanding; that's how we can serve God and others first. When the Lord is our number-one priority, His values become our values. We will always be compelled to love and serve as He does when we put Him first! This is a blessing and ministry not only to the Lord, but to the people around us.

Discussion Questions

1. How can God occupy the first place in our hearts alongside other areas of our calling?

_____

_____

_____

_____

_____

_____

_____

_____

_____

_____

2. Why is it problematic to compartmentalize areas of our life? For example, why is our ministry not more important than our family?

_____

_____

_____

_____

_____

_____

_____

_____

_____

3. How would your life change if you truly believed every area of your days could be an offering the Lord?

_____

_____

_____

_____

_____

_____

_____

_____

_____

_____

4. Just as importantly, how would culture shift if you believed this?

_____

_____

_____

_____

_____

_____

_____

_____

_____

Solomon and Queen Sheba

Pastor Bill shared a profound scriptural example of how our passion and purpose can fuel Kingdom advancement. When Solomon built a beautiful staircase to Heaven, Queen Sheba was so impressed that she came to know the Lord! In the same way, our acts of faithfulness, excellence, and creativity can inspire others to know God.

1. How, specifically, does our excellence and creativity display God to the world?

_____

_____

_____

_____

_____

_____

_____

_____

2. What are a few ways your own work, whether in the home, in a hobby, or in your job, could be an example of who God is to others?

_____

Activation: Building Your Stairway

Take time together as small groups and talk about Solomon's staircase that Pastor Bill shared.

What is one thing you took away from that story? Did anything surprise you? What encouraged or challenged you?

As you reflect on the idea that there is no "ordinary" area of life, pray over one another. Ask God to empower your group members to take joy in the mundane of their days so they can experience and display God's Kingdom in a new way.

Video Listening Guide Answer Key:

1. Number one, number two

2. Worship

3. Life

4. God

5. Ordinary

Good job! We are hopeful that you will continue to hear from God over the next two weeks.

Session Eight

THE KINGDOM OF ABUNDANCE

It's important not to mix up "church values" with "Kingdom culture." While we are called to see a continual increase of glory in the church, the church is supposed to influence the world in a positive and measurable way. Heaven on Earth is essentially the governmental influence of another world being released into this one, and the Lord wants to empower us to impact every aspect of culture with His culture.

JOURNAL

Week 8

VIDEO LISTENING GUIDE

1. "Evil" comes from a word that means "_____" or "_____."

2. The redemptive work of Jesus broke the back of _____, _____, and _____.

3. God wants us to prosper physically and materially, just as our _____ prosper.

4. The Kingdom of God must first manifest as an _____ reality.

5. Still, Kingdom abundance impacts the _____ realm.

Summary

God's heart is for our abundance. Material wealth is not the goal of walking with God. He calls us to internal abundance first and foremost. Still, our internal abundance can manifest in physical abundance, which brings the Kingdom into our lives further. He is a good Father, and He wants His children to prosper, mind, body, and soul!

Jesus' Redemptive Work

The work of Jesus on the cross is the foundation of our abundance. In John 10:10, we read that Jesus came to give us abundant life! Without His sacrifice, we would not have access to health and prosperity, the hallmarks of God's Kingdom.

Discussion Questions

1. What did Jesus' death accomplish for us in terms of securing our abundance?

_____

_____

_____

_____

_____

_____

_____

2. How can we live in our destiny when we are free from sin, disease, and poverty?

3. What does it say about the Lord that He desires His children's abundance and prosperity?

_____

_____

_____

_____

_____

_____

_____

_____

Internal and External Abundance

Sometimes, our physical problems can have spiritual roots. That's why it's so important to align our souls with God's values. When we repent and move toward Him, He renews our hearts, making room for us to experience abundance and health in every way.

1. Why is it so important that we focus on our internal abundance first?

_____

_____

_____

_____

_____

_____

_____

_____

_____

_____

_____

2. What role does self-talk play in our prosperity?

_____

_____

_____

_____

_____

_____

_____

_____

_____

3. What does it mean that the "creative role of every believer is being restored"?

_____

_____

_____

_____

_____

_____

_____

_____

_____

_____

_____

Activation: Avenues of Abundance

Take time as individuals and reflect on how God might want to bring abundance into your life. Is there an area where you need freedom or blessing?

Pray into this part of your life, expectant that God will not only deliver you, but bless you.

If you are struggling to believe God will come through for you, reflect on John 10:10. Focus on remembering who Jesus is and what He came to do for you, God's child.

After you pray, journal about three ways you can pursue this abundance personally.

Then get in groups of two and share the three things you journaled about and pray over each other to have grace to pursue those three areas.

Video Listening Guide Answer Key

1. Pain or poverty

2. Sin, disease, poverty

3. Souls

4. Internal

5. Material

Thank you so much for partnering with us for the past eight weeks. We are so thankful you joined us, and we pray God ignites you with His love for a life of passion and power!

NOTES

NOTES

NOTES

NOTES

NOTES

NOTES

NOTES

NOTES

NOTES

NOTES

Looking for more from Bill Johnson?

Purchase additional resources—CDs, DVDs, digital downloads, music—from Bill Johnson at bethel.store.

Visit bjm.org for more information on Bill Johnson, to view his speaking itinerary, or to look into additional teaching resources.

Become part of a Supernatural Culture that is transforming the world and *apply* to the Bethel School of Supernatural Ministry: bssm.net.

For more information, visit bethel.com.

OTHER CURRICULUM AVAILABLE FROM BILL JOHNSON AND THE BETHEL TEAM

THE SUPERNATURAL POWER OF A TRANSFORMED MIND
CURRICULUM

"A WAKE-UP CALL TO THE 'GREATER THINGS THAN THESE SHALL YOU DO' PROMISE OF JESUS." - RANDY CLARK

In *Supernatural Power of a Transformed Mind*, Pastor Bill Johnson delivers powerful and practical teaching, revealing how you were designed to bring heaven to Earth and how it all starts with your thought life.

Your access to a lifestyle of signs, wonders, and miracles starts by changing the way you think. When your mind is transformed, heaven becomes more than a place you go to one day—it becomes the supernatural power that you release wherever you go today!

INCLUDED IN THIS CURRICULUM:

DVD Study and Leader's Guide • Study Guide • *Supernatural Power of a Transformed Mind* Book

BILL JOHNSON
GOD is GOOD
CURRICULUM

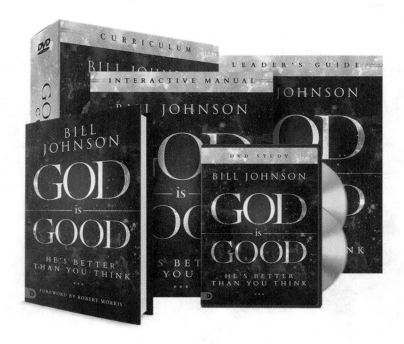

Your View of God Impacts Everything

"God is Good." More than a positive thought, theological concept, or Biblical statement—what you do with these three words defines your reality and determines your destiny.

Ideal for small groups, church classes, and personal study, *God is Good* features 8 dynamic DVD sessions recorded live at Bethel Church and 8 weeks of powerful, interactive discipleship training. Learn how to:

- Clearly discern the difference between the will of God and the enemy's plans.
- Confidently pray for breakthrough, believe for miracles, and have faith for God to move, no matter what comes against you.
- Find rest in God's unchanging character and embrace the value of mystery... even when prayers aren't immediately answered.
- Discover God's goodness in both Old and New Testaments.
- Encounter Jesus Christ as perfect theology—the One who reveals a good Father.
- Partner with Heaven to release supernatural solutions to a world in chaos.

Curriculum Box Set Includes
God is Good book, 2-Disk DVD Set (8 Sessions), Leader's Guide, Interactive Manual
(course components also sold separately)

Encounter God like never before!

HOSTING *the* PRESENCE

SPECIAL PRICING ON STUDY KITS

Home Study • Small Group • Large Group

www.hostingthepresence.com

 **Destiny Image**

CALL 1.800.722.6774
www.DestinyImage.com

Healthy & Free

A JOURNEY TO WELLNESS FOR YOUR BODY, SOUL, AND SPIRIT

Experience Heaven's Health!

Beni Johnson received a life-changing revelation about how anyone can start walking in holistic health—including you! Jesus died for your spirit, soul, and body. This means you can experience His resurrection life in all three areas!

Christians should be the healthiest people on earth because they understand God has made their bodies His temple. Unfortunately, many people focus on one area of health while neglecting the others. This can lead to spiritual disconnection, bad eating habits, depression, poor rest, and lack of exercise.

In the *Healthy and Free* video curriculum, Beni personally teaches you how to:

- **Find your why:** Learn the motivating secret to pursuing a healthy lifestyle as your new normal.
- **Unlock the connection:** Discover the many ways your spirit, soul, and body are interconnected and how health in one area directly affects another.
- **Start simple:** Receive practical and easy-to-implement steps to begin walking in health right now.

The Great Physician desires you to walk in Heaven's health. Get aligned with God's divine design today and experience freedom—body, soul, and spirit!

INCLUDED IN THIS CURRICULUM:
8-Session DVD Study • Leader's Guide • Study Guide • *Healthy and Free* Book

Experience a personal revival!

Spirit-empowered content from today's top Christian authors delivered directly to your inbox.

Join today!
lovetoreadclub.com

Inspiring Articles

Powerful Video Teaching

Resources for Revival

Get all of this and so much more, e-mailed to you twice weekly!

LOVE TO READ CLUB

by **D** DESTINY IMAGE